A MACDONALD BOOK

Text © 1988 Angela Littler
Illustrations © 1988 Macdonald & Co (Publishers) Ltd

First published in Great Britain in 1988
by Macdonald & Co (Publishers) Ltd
London & Sydney

A member of Maxwell Pergamon Publishing Corporation plc

Printed and bound in Spain by Cronion S.A.

ISBN 0 356 13498 9
ISBN 0 356 16032 7 pbk

Macdonald & Co (Publishers) Ltd
Greater London House
Hampstead Road
London NW1 7QX

Tasting and Smelling

Written by Angela Littler

Illustrated by Corinne Burrows

Macdonald

Smelling

This is my nose. It helps me to breathe and to smell things.

My nostrils have hairs and sticky stuff in them to trap the dirt.

A special place deep behind my nose smells the smells for me. It is called the nasal cavity.

I breathe air in through my nostrils. Smells come in with the air.

I blow my nose to get rid of the dirt in it.

Sometimes my nose makes me sneeze out anything it does not like.

I sniff hard to smell something I like. The sniff takes the air right up into the smelling part of my nose.

5

Tasting

This is my tongue. It helps me to talk, to eat and to taste things.

The little pimples all over my tongue are full of tiny taste buds. Taste buds help me to taste things that are sweet, salty, sour and bitter.

I taste bitter things at the back of my tongue.

I taste sour things on the sides of my tongue.

I taste sweet and salty things on the tip of my tongue.

The watery stuff in my mouth is called saliva. It wets my food as I eat. When I smell good things, my mouth waters. It is getting ready to eat.

Tasting and smelling go together. When I have a cold and my nose blocks up, I cannot smell or taste anything.

Animal facts

The skunk uses a
horrible smelly spray
to get rid of its enemies.
The smell lasts for days.

Ants leave a smelly trail to lead other ants to food.

Tom cats use a
bad-smelling spray to
label a place as their
own. The smell tells
other toms to keep
away.

8

Dogs have a very powerful sense of smell and are used to sniff out drugs and guns.

Sharks can smell blood in the water from a long way off. Divers sometimes carry a special spray to keep them away.

What smells?

Some things smell strongly. Some things do not smell at all. Sometimes we smell pleasant smells. Sometimes we smell bad ones. Which of these things smell good to you? Which things smell bad? Which things have no smell? What is your favourite smell?

A smelly puzzle

Imagine that you have no sense of smell. There are seven strong smells in this picture that you would not be able to notice. Can you spot them? Which are the two warning smells?

A. 1. New-mown grass. 2. Roses. 3. Burning pan of milk. 4. Cakes burning in oven. 5. Cheese . 6. Perfume . 7. Onion.

Kinds of tastes

These things taste either sweet, sour, salty or bitter on our tongues. Can you think of more?

sweet

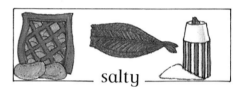

salty

sour

bitter

Next time you have an orange, or a lemon slice, or a crisp, or a chocolate, hold your nose and see which part of your tongue tastes it best. Then check here and on page 6 to see whether the taste was sweet, salty, sour or bitter.

Taste buds game

For two players

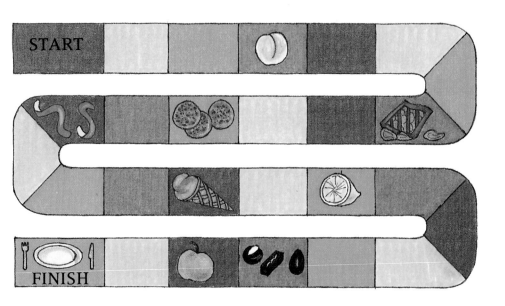

You will need a die and two counters. Take turns
to throw the die and move your counters. If you
land on a food picture you must say if the food
tastes sweet, sour, salty or bitter. If you are right
take an extra go. The first player to reach the plate
on the table wins the game.

13

Make a lavender bag

You can put lavender bags in clothes drawers to make them scented.

Use thin cotton material or two layers of net for your lavender bag. You will also need some dried lavender, and about 50cm of very thin ribbon.

Find a small plate to use as a pattern, some scissors or pinking shears and a pencil.

1. Put the plate face down on the material. Draw round it with a pencil to make a circle.

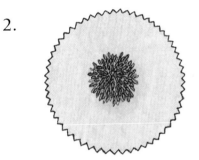

2. Cut out the circle of material. Use pinking shears if you can, to give a pretty zig-zag edge. Put a little pile of dried lavender in the middle.

3. Tie the lavender up in the bag very tightly with the ribbon.

Tasty treats

Here are some delicious treats for you to make and eat.

Banana Popsicles

1. For two popsicles, peel a banana and cut it in half.

1.

2. Push an ice lolly stick or half a plastic straw gently into each bit of banana.

2.

3. Coat each banana in hundreds-and-thousands, or chocolate strands. Put the bananas in the freezer for two hours.

3.

Tutti Fruttis

1. Peel and cut some fruit into very small pieces.

1.

2. Put two or three pieces of fruit in each little square of an ice-cube tray.

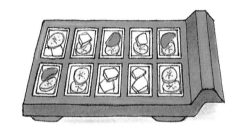
2.

3. Make up some blackcurrant drink. Pour it into the ice-cube tray. Put the tray in the freezer until the tutti fruttis are frozen.

3.

17

Peanut Butter Chomps

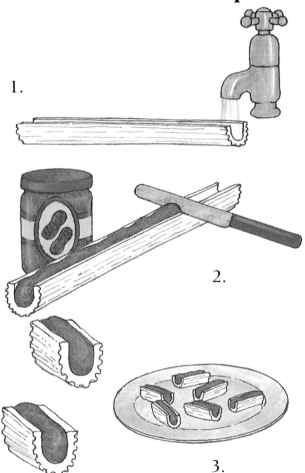

1.

2.

3.

1. Wash a stick of celery well.

2. Spread the hollow inside of the celery with peanut butter.

3. Cut the celery into bite-size pieces.

Peppermint Fondants

1. In a basin, mix about four tablespoons of icing sugar with about two teaspoons of water. Add one drop of green food colouring and one drop of peppermint essence.

1.

2. Dust your hands with icing sugar. Roll little balls of the fondant mixture. Put them on greaseproof paper.

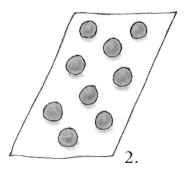

2.

3. Flatten the balls with the palm of your hand. Decorate with silver balls or walnut pieces. Leave for a few hours in a dry place to harden.

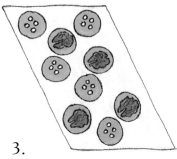

3.

A smelly story

Look at the picture opposite.

Tom and his mother and sister were going for a picnic by the sea. It was a fine day, so the car windows were open. They let in all sorts of interesting smells.

Soon after they left home, there was the strong smell of petrol, as Tom's mother filled up the car. Off they went, but they soon had to slow down. Tom could smell the fumes of a traffic jam. He closed the window until they were moving again.

Tom smelled the scent of flowers and looked up. He saw trees full of blossom. They turned a corner and passed a delicious smell of food cooking on a barbecue.

A Smelly Journey

Read the story on page 20 and 22, and see if you can work out which way Tom's car went on its journey. Then work out some smelly journeys for yourself.

Suddenly, there was the strong, tangy smell of the sea. They had arrived! They had a tasty picnic. Then they splashed in the sea and made sandcastles. All too soon, it was time to go home.

On the way back, they passed a fishy smell coming from a market stall.

Tom and his sister were getting hungry now. Suddenly, there was a mouth-watering smell of food frying. Their mother stopped and bought them hamburgers and chips for supper.

Then they drove straight home tired and sleepy after a day full of different smells and tastes.